[Handwritten inscription:]
Judith,
As Lucille's spirit,
both bless you.
love for you. Let wisdom be your guide.
Shalom,
Dr. Val
4.18.21

LEADING FROM THE INSIDE OUT: DAILY
WISDOM FOR COMPASSIONATE LEADERS

---

*"For I know the plans I have for you," says the Lord.
"They are plans for good and not disaster, to give you a
future and a hope." (Jeremiah 29:11)*

Dr. Valmarie Rhoden

[Signature:] Dr. Valmarie Ward Rhoden

Leading from the Inside Out: Daily Wisdom for Compassionate Leaders
Copyright © 2020 Dr. Valmarie Rhoden

ISBN: 978-0-578-83208-1.
But First Jesus Ministries, Inc.

Preface

Beloved, this book is the manifestation of a divine dream built on the promises of God. I have spent most of my life in a leadership role from assisting my kindergarten teacher in our one-room schoolhouse with lunch distribution and "taking names" when she had to leave the classroom for a quick minute. Now I know I'm dating myself by using the expression, "taking names." For my millennial readers, this simply means noting who misbehaved. I hope that helps and it's no problem if you can't envision yourself learning in a one-room schoolhouse. Trust me—it was effective; and I will guide you through other confirming experiences.

Throughout my formal education, including Graduate School and Seminary, I found myself or was called to stand and lead. Moreover, the experience that challenged me most was my seven years as a high school principal. It is from that experience this book was born. Scholars have forever debated whether leaders are born or nurtured. I believe leaders are called and ordained to bear fruit, and their fruit will remain (John 15:16). Leaders are created from their daily experiences that form them from the inside out. Many days as a principal, I felt alone and without hope. There were demands on every side from superiors, staff, students, parents, and the community. Many days it was the small voice of a student saying, "Thank you, Ms. Rhoden," that kept me going.

Today, I realize I was not alone—I had not been forgotten. The many times I drew on what I thought was my own strength, I was really drawing from the well of strength of the Holy Spirit. From inside of me, I found the wisdom to answer the demands and the kindness to grant the wishes of the small voices of my students, who I loved beyond measure. Yet, my physical energy and health suffered. I was stricken with Bell's Palsy, and the doctor said the cause was probably stress. However, I was supernaturally healed as a Pastor friend stopped to pray for me in her hair salon. No matter how stressful it got throughout those seven years as principal, I never lost my will for excellence in all things and compassion for others. I believe, and I hope that after reading this book, you will too.

My hope as a leader has been in the Lord. From the inside out, He is transforming me through His Word to be a light in this dark world. In this world, many seem to be more concerned with the things that satisfy the flesh only. But I offer this book to leaders from all walks of life and to people whose hearts have become hardened by the cares of this world and by those who have helped and harmed them. Through this little manual of guideposts, I hope to reach those who are driven by pain, greed, strife, jealousy, and self-centeredness. It is my prayer, they too, will be transformed from the inside out.

This pocket manual gives you 30 days of truth to apply to everyday life. What is truth? Truth is the Word of God. Jesus, in his priestly prayer in John 17:17, asked the Father to sanctify His disciples by the truth, for your word is truth.

I remember distinctly one day as principal a student spoke words into my spirit that changed me forever. I was known to shed tears of joy and pain quite often. I guess I was like Jeremiah, the weeping prophet. But on that day I was apologizing to a student for crying (not sure about what), and she said, "Don't worry, Ms. Rhoden, your tears baptize us." Those words struck me like a lightning bolt or colliding ships, and I never apologized again. May this book born from my tears and joys baptize you with the faith to know the Father has an expected end of peace for you. May the wisdom guideposts navigate you into safe harbor. You are never alone--let your leadership experiences transform you from the inside out.

Dr. Val

Dedication
To my Heavenly Father

You never forgot me; You never left me alone,

Thank you.

You created me to lead with a servant's heart,

Thank you.

You blessed me to be a blessing to others,

Thank you.

I am love because you love me,

Thank you.

You sanctified me with your truth,

Bless you.

To my Earthly Parents
Valder Eddie and Willie Ann Ward,

I know Christ because of your example,

Thank you.

I know the power of prayer because of you,

Thank you.

I have strength in knowing I can do all things

through Christ by your teachings

Thank you.

I know Christ will bless the work of my hands

because you taught me work is honorable,

I honor you.

To my Sons (my seeds)
Edward and Christopher

I pray you will grow to know the Father more intimately.

The more you know Him, the more you will love and obey Him.

I love you beyond measure.

Mom

Table of Contents

Introduction

This wisdom manual is written during a time of great unrest in America. The violent overtaking of the U.S. Capitol, and the killings of Brown and Black men across the country stream across every news show. The retaliatory slaughter of five Dallas, Texas police officers while they rushed toward the gunmen to protect peaceful protestors of the Black Lives Matter Movement grips the hearts of all America. Yes, and the most contentious Presidential race in history will leave an indelible scar. What do we expect our leaders in Law Enforcement, Government, and the Church to do during these turbulent times?

Leaders in all walks of life sometimes find themselves searching for supernatural solutions to natural problems. I am reminded of when Peter and his buddies were fishing all night and caught nothing. In John 21:6, we read where God commanded them to throw their nets on the right side of the boat where they would be more successful; and indeed, their nets were full of a great catch. Peter did the natural, and a supernatural solution manifested. This manual is written to believers and non-believers in Christ to till the soil of your hearts to receive the seed (Word of God) so that it can grow and bring forth a great catch that will multiply and last in your churches, schools, or any organization.

How to Use this Wisdom Manual

Y ou will get the most out of this guidebook by keeping it in your pocket, purse, or on top of your desk for quick access. Open to any page whenever you face a problem or challenge, read, and meditate on the wisdom nugget provided. Be still and listen for the Holy Spirit to whisper God's Word into your heart. Go to the journal note section and briefly write how you will apply what you discerned. This is not written as a daily devotional. This is a companion guide to the Word of God that will draw you into a more intimate relationship with God. From this relationship, you will receive wisdom, knowledge, and ideas to strengthen your leadership experience and to be a greater blessing to those you serve. Could you read it daily? Should you read it year after year? Of course, each entry is divinely inspired by the Holy Spirit. All Scripture is God-breathed and is profitable for teaching, rebuking, correcting, and training any day of the year (2 Timothy 3:16).

The principle of leading from the inside out is a supernatural way to create an inspiring vision and to motivate others to reach that vision. As I look back over my years of struggle as a school principal, I realize there were no problems or questions that Christ had not answered in His Word. I realize I was not alone—the Holy Spirit was there all the time quietly guiding me. I want my readers to know this now! So, I share 30 days of wisdom to encourage your hearts, to improve your leadership experience, and to let you know you are not alone. It is my prayer that this companion guide to the Bible will enable you to lead others to the marvelous light of the Father's Kingdom. Whether you believe it or not—the Word still works. You owe it to yourself and those you serve to add this manual to your arsenal of leadership resources. I assure you this is like none other! May you be divinely blessed as you take this journey to a more intimate relationship with the Creator. I believe leaders armed with the Word of God can change the trajectory of an organization and this country.

I have divided this wisdom manual into four main parts. This first part deals with the force of wisdom that is available to everyone. I want to firmly establish in your hearts that no man needs to feel alone or feel like a failure because the wisdom of God is at your disposal. All Scriptures are taken from the New King James Version of the Bible.

"Lessons in life will be repeated until they
are learned."
Frank Sonnenberg

Part I
The Force of Wisdom

Y ou don't have to possess great eyesight to have great vision. You simply must seek wisdom and guidance from the Holy Spirit. When you partner with Him to lead from the inside out, you make courageous choices. You live fully filled with excitement and intrigue for what the future holds for you and those in your care. Then, you look for blessings in all circumstances. When you lead from the inside out, you see life and work as Christ sees them. You are aligned with the mind of Christ (I Corinthians 2:16).

The Book of Proverbs contains short, truthful statements about how we behave as humans; and written primarily to instruct us of the consequences. It is best known as the Wisdom Book.

The Benefits of Wisdom

My child, listen to what I say,

and treasure my commands.

Tune your ears to wisdom,

and concentrate on understanding.

Cry out for insight,

and ask for understanding.

Search for them as you would for silver;

seek them like hidden treasures.

Then you will understand what it means to fear the Lord,

and you will gain knowledge of God.

For the Lord grants wisdom!

From his mouth come knowledge and understanding.

He grants a treasure of common sense to the honest.

He is a shield to those who walk with integrity.

He guards the paths of the just

and protects those who are faithful to him.

Then you will understand what is right, just, and fair,

and you will find the right way to go.

For wisdom will enter your heart,

and knowledge will fill you with joy.

Wise choices will watch over you.

Understanding will keep you safe.

Wisdom will save you from evil people,

from those whose words are twisted. (Proverbs 2:1-12)

Wisdom Guidepost #1 – What is Wisdom
Proverbs 2:6

For the Lord gives wisdom; from his mouth come knowledge and understanding

Did you take driver's education in high school or taught your child to drive? Then you're probably familiar with the acronym S-I-P-D-E. The letters stand for Scan, Identify, Predict, Decide, and Execute. On any given day when it seems that roadblocks are at every turn—down every hallway or present in every meeting, you can translate these words to your professional and spiritual growth. Just take a deep breath and scan the environment, identify the hazards or roadblocks, predict what the hazards or roadblocks might do, decide how to respond, and then, if necessary, execute that plan. Remember, You do not have to respond immediately or at all to every hazard or roadblock. Be wise in choosing your battles. Choosing your battles means to be selective of the problems, arguments, and confrontations you get involved in. Fight what's most important and let go of the rest!

Wisdom Guidepost #2- Simply Ask
James 1:5-6

If any of you lacks wisdom, let him ask of God, who gives to liberally and without reproach, and it will be given to him. But let him ask in faith, with no doubting, for he who doubts is like a wave of the sea driven and tossed by the wind.

Today, I hope you awoke with the intention to have a good day. Like me, I proclaim each morning that great things are going to happen for me this day and through me for others. But then you walk out of your house and into the world! The first trial comes, and you can stand on the words you spoke at home, and all is well. But after about the third trial, your patience and strength are nearly exhausted. What should you do? Simply ask for wisdom. James is teaching you to be joyful even amid troubles. It is in that space where you experience God's grace. It is here where patience will win over frustration and spiritual strength over anger.

Find space and time to go before the Father and tell Him how you're feeling. This will give you a more objective view of the situation and allow you to exhale. Then listen for guidance and act upon it ASAP. Today is the day you will push aside your own understanding and usual reactions and seek the wisdom of God. Most important, today, you commit to obey!

Wisdom Guidepost #3-The Wise Builder
Matthew 7:24-25

Therefore, whosoever hears these sayings of Mine, and does them, I will liken him to a wise man who built his house upon a rock: and the rain descended, the floods came, and the winds blew, and beat on that house; and it did not fall, for it was founded on the rock.

As a leader, you are a vision builder. The Parable of the Builder introduces you to two types of builders. One who is wise hears and acts according to the guidance of the Holy Spirit; and the other foolish, who hears and continues to act on his own knowledge. Today, through leading from the inside out, you will be known as a wise builder. Like me, you have probably tried to solve the daily challenges of leading with strategies that didn't work or simply masked the real issue. Haven't we heard time and time again that insanity is doing the same thing the same way and expecting a different result? To get something different, you must do something different; and that is be led by the Spirit. Being led by the Spirit does not make you weak or less authoritative. Your true authority comes from within— your intimate relationship with the Father.

You were given the authority to be fruitful and to have dominion (authority) in Genesis 1:28. You were created in the image of God (the Imago Dei) and blessed to succeed in what you put your hands to. So, stop trying to go it alone. Yield to your divine nature and lead with confidence and calm resolve that you are a wise builder with a direct connection to the Source of all wisdom. Leading from the inside out won't happen overnight, but don't give up. Little by little, it will become your go-to strategy that will change your entire environment.

Wisdom Guidepost #4-Wisdom, Understanding and Knowledge
Exodus 31:1-3

Then the Lord said to Moses, saying: "See I have
called by name Bezalel the son of Uri, the son of Hur,
of the tribe of
Judah: And I have filled him with the Spirit of God,
in wisdom,
in understanding, in knowledge, and in
all manner of workmanship.

When you are in the middle of a leadership challenge, it may feel like pushing a boulder up a steep hill. You may say there is no way I can do this. Stop that right now! Your words are carriers of powerful forces of blessing or curse. In the beginning, God spoke everything into existence. He said, "Let there be light and there was light." Remember from Wisdom Guidepost #3, you are made in His image. Therefore, you can speak things into existence as well. So, can I get you to agree to only speak words of blessing? Now, you have the knowledge and understanding to move that leadership challenge that seemed to be the size of a boulder. You can, but only by leading from the inside out. How is it done? Let me give you an illustration from the Old Testament.

When craftsmen were needed to build the Tabernacle, the Lord told Moses He had chosen and filled Bezalel with the Spirit of God giving him great wisdom, ability, and expertise in all kinds of crafts. The same applies to you. You are equipped from the inside out to be a great problem solver, a boulder mover, and great builder. When fear, doubt, and insecurity try to creep into your mind, say this, "I am an astute problem solver and a wise builder."

Wisdom Guidepost #5-You are not Alone
Isaiah 41:10

Fear not, for I am with you: Be not dismayed, for I am your God. I will strengthen you, Yes, I will help you. I will uphold you with my righteous right hand.

Leadership, I know, can be a lonely place to be. So many people are demanding your time and energy. So little energy being returned to feed your inner man or woman. Many things being thrown at you at once—the voices seem limitless and synchronized. Did these people get together and plan their personal, simultaneous attacks? In some cases, yes, but most likely, it's just par for the course. During these lonesome times, you need to hear an assuring voice that you are not alone, and someone cares. Have you ever heard God speaking to you? Was it a loud audible voice or was it a quiet stirring in your soul (your mind, will, and emotions)? If you have never heard from God, listen to His tender words recorded by the Prophet Isaiah. Fear not, for I am with you! This short phrase is a calming assurance that not only is God within hearing distance, but He is also present with you. If you are weak, draw on His mighty strength. If you feel defenseless to shoulder the demands of life and work, God is your ever-present help. When you feel you're at the end of your rope and about to let go, hold on to His mighty right hand. No matter what you are going through at this moment, know you are not alone, and this too shall pass.

This feeling of being alone was a constant source of angst for me as the principal of a large inner-city high school. So, please allow me to dive deeper into this wisdom signpost. I use the growth of the giant redwood tree to reveal we are not created to experience life and leadership alone. The redwood can best be described as immense, ancient, stately, mysterious, and powerful. Their existence speaks for themselves—with patient endurance over the many years of their life cycle, much like the Holy Spirit, who is patient with you and directs you in quiet peace. The massive redwood from a seed the size of a tomato can grow to 367 feet with a width of 22 feet at the base. But despite its massive size, the redwood root system only goes down 10 to 13 feet before spreading outward. The roots are spreading outward to connect with those of other redwoods. This is why you rarely see a redwood standing alone. The same holds true for leaders. The freedom to lead effectively comes through relationships. Don't be deceived in believing that if you pour your heart, soul, and strength into work, you will be fulfilled and a successful leader. You, like the redwood, were not created to experience life and work alone. Let the Holy Spirit guide you to fulfillment and peace. Let those in your care be your connecting roots, so you all stand tall and strong together!

"A goal is a statement of faith."
Rick Warren

Wisdom Guidepost #6- Use Your Imagination
2 Corinthians 9:8

And God is able to make all grace abound toward
you, that you, always having all sufficiency in all
things, may have an abundance for every good work.

D o you sometimes get frustrated by what you view
as a lack of progress in your career, personal
projects, or ministry? Do you see others who are less
qualified being promoted and revered? Have you

witnessed the ministries of those not as gifted or anointed growing in number and outreach? And you sit and ask why you are not prospering. I want you to use your imagination to shatter those negative images and visualize yourself as you want to be. Use your imagination and be transformed, especially when you combine it with spirituality. As rewarding as using your imagination can be, it may be difficult for some. But hear me, you must press your way through those old images of doubt, fear, and even covetousness (desiring what belongs to others). When you do, you make room for confidence, fresh ideas, and new projects. Be patient as transformation takes time... but it will happen.

Carolina Herrera, a Venezuelan fashion designer, known for exceptional personal style, said it this way, "Balance is always found in discipline." Use your imagination and discipline yourself to set faith goals to achieve your personal and professional goals. A goal is a statement of faith (Rick Warren). The prayer of Jabez can be the catalyst for moving to the next level in leadership. Jabez called on the God of Israel, saying, "Oh, that you would bless me indeed, and enlarge my territory, that your hand will be with me, and that you would keep me from evil that I may not cause pain (I Chronicles 4:10)!" God granted him what he requested. Like Jabez, God will smile favorably on your faith goals as well.

Rick Warren describes faith goals like this:

F=Focused

A=Attainable

I=Individual

T=Trackable

H=Heartfelt

The goals must be specific, practical, personal, measurable, and passionate. Faith goals give life to your dreams, so if you're not passionate about them, forget them! Faith goals with the leading of the Holy Spirit can provide illumination during dark times in leadership. I've been there, and I know! They can give you inner strength and confidence to move forward without fear or concern. You become more conscious of God's direction, leading you to wise choices and wisdom to traverse the chopping waters of leadership. God gave Solomon wisdom and exceedingly great understanding, and largeness of heart like the sand on the seashore" (I Kings 4:29). Solomon's life is the lens through which you can view wisdom and prudence. Study I Kings and the glorious history of how Solomon's faith moved mountains and how, with wisdom, he built temples. There is a "Solomon" inside of you to lead from the inside out!

"A compassionate leader cannot impose his will on others; but must search for goals that are compatible with everyone."

Bass & Steidlmeier

Wisdom Guidepost #7-Write the Vision
Habakkuk 2:2-3

Then the Lord answered me and said: "Write the vision and make it plain on tablets, That he may run who reads it. For the vision is yet for an appointed time; but at the end it will speak; and it will not lie. Though it tarries, wait for it; Because it will surely come, it will not tarry.

Great eyesight is not a requirement to have great vision; but you must write the vision down. A steady stream of studies of effective leadership has been done in recent decades—Kouzes and Posner and Bennis and Nanus in 2007 (framework for my dissertation), to name two. The universal characteristic of these studies is vision and focus. Effective leaders help articulate a vision, set standards for performance, and create focus and direction. A characteristic related to vision and focus is effective communication. Another quality often mentioned in leadership research is commitment or passion. Remember, the fifth descriptor of a faith goal in Wisdom Guidepost #7 is heartfelt! Compassionate leaders who lead from the inside out care deeply about their work and the people who work alongside them. They inspire trust and build authenticity based on trust.

But let's be honest. Despite your best efforts, you will have dissenters. Judges 21:25 recounts a time when there was no king in Israel, and everyone did what was right in their own eyes. Leaders, therefore, must be able to effectively communicate vision and to keep everyone focused on the goals. Inside out, leaders realize they are not independent actors; they both shape and are shaped by their constituents (Gardner, 1989). As a compassionate leader, you cannot impose your will on others; but must search for goals that are compatible with everyone (Bass & Steidlmeier, 1999). Proverbs 27:17 teaches us that iron sharpens iron—everyone becomes wiser and better by working together.

Seek guidance from other compassionate leaders in developing and writing your vision. Don't try to redirect God's will or compete with others. You know that late arrival does not mean failure. God's Will is about more than your temporary circumstances, it's about eternity. More failure can come from an excess of caution than from boldly implementing your vision.

Wisdom Guidepost #8-Start with Prayer
Ephesians 1:16-17

I do not cease to give thanks for you, making mention of you in my prayers: that the God of our Lord Jesus Christ, the Father of glory, may give to you the spirit of wisdom and revelation in the knowledge of Him.

As a compassionate leader you are challenged each day to make wise decisions that align with corporate guidelines and structure. It matters not whether you are a spiritual leader or not—pray first!

Prayer takes self-discipline, but that discipline will saturate other areas of your life. Beware that it is when you are most disinclined to pray that you most need to do so. Prayer will give you a new direction and a new vitality. You can pray in your office, in the classroom or boardroom. No one has to know what you are doing. Have you ever noticed a turning wheel has obvious movement from the outside, but the center seems to remain still? You too, can quiet yourself inwardly and be centered with the Spirit of God. Take this small step of connecting from within each day, and you will find yourself poised to make wise decisions without fear of conflict or rejection. This is a 2 for 1—you are at peace and aligned with your personal values and virtues.

When you lead from the inside out, you will not lose yourself. You can courageously be yourself and serve others with the fullness of who you are—your passions, values, and virtues. This prayer, paraphrased from Mary Ellen Simpson, is available to you:

Lord, give me the Courage to be myself …

To know I am not alone

God and I are one—Together

Lord, give me the Courage to be myself …

To shine my light, to cast out fears,

and to take a chance to be me.

"Never mistake knowledge for wisdom. One helps you make a living; the other helps you make a life."
Sandra Carey

Part 2 – Wisdom for the Day-to-Day Journey

I chuckled many years ago when I heard someone say if you look behind you and no one is there, you're not leading. Who's benefitting from your leadership? Leading from the inside out leads to freedom for others to achieve their faith goals as well. Positive relationships lift you higher to connect with your vision—it's a win/win endeavor. From the summit of a hill or mountain, a new panorama view appears. From this new perspective, your vision is clearer, with less obstruction. You are now free to choose and explore new territory. This new vista is where you can be guided in building and nurturing mutually beneficial relationships. Colossians 3:10 calls a leader at this point, a new man who is renewed in the knowledge according to the image of Him who created you.

Always place a high value on your relationships. Their value is greater than gold. Maya Angelou, the great African American poet, said, "I've learned people will forget what you said, people will forget what you did, but people will never forget how you made them feel." Inside out, leaders come alongside people with compassion. They ask questions and really listen. They truly believe that the people on their team might have viable solutions not previously considered. They come alongside those they lead to be of help and to be helped by them. They speak and listen; they teach and learn.

Leading from the inside out is more challenging today than ever. There are so many distractors that keep you from focusing on the vision and your faith goals. The work we do, whether in a school, the marketplace or in a congregation, is done with lightning speed and on a global basis. The Internet and social media are kings. Though the climate for leaders has changed, the challenge of compassionate leadership remains the same. How do we get the best possible results from those we serve? Leadership at the core is pursuing more productive interactions between individuals. Compassionate leaders find the best ways to communicate and come alongside others from moment to moment to build relationships that are enduring and high performing. This is tough I know but check out these other wisdom guideposts.

Wisdom Guidepost #9- Inevitability of Opposition
Luke 12:11-12

"Now when they bring you to the synagogues and magistrates and authorities, do not worry about how or what you should answer, or what you should say. For the Holy Spirit will teach you in that very hour what you ought to say."

A vast crowd gathered to hear Christ teach, but the scribes and Pharisees sought to accuse Him because of jealousy and prejudice. They sought to ensnare Him, but the stronger their opposition, the more the people flocked to hear the words of wisdom. Opposition to leadership is not new and will not go away quietly into the night. Nietzsche, German philosopher, and poet believed life always gets harder toward the summit. The cold gets colder, the wind stronger, the burden of responsibility heavier. Compassionate leaders, therefore, welcome support from others but have sufficient inner resources to stand alone—even in the face of inflexible opposition.

Opposition as a leader may be done in an open or closed-door manner. Know whether your accusers are overt or covert in their actions, their purpose is the same—to intimidate, silence and render you ineffective. Some will try you in the "Court of Public Opinion." They may encircle you with rapid-fire questioning. They carefully craft their questions to snare you into contradicting your word or policy. But compassionate leaders who lead from the inside out can turn the table on their accusers. So, don't cower in fear. Stand firmly and provide bold and direct answers to their contrived questions. Caveat Emptor, Latin for let the buyer beware, is appropriate at this point. Opposition can come from unlikely sources, those who appear to be a supportive member of your team. So, beware! The reasons for opposition are numerous and vary from person to person. Yet, be selective in how you address each attack. Disobey only in specific instances where to obey would violate your moral principles and values. As compassionate leaders, we do not leave our moral principles and values at the front door. Be your authentic self. Be honest and forthright about what you will and will not do. Stand on the truth of the Word of God. Let the Holy Spirit be your guide, and victory is ahead.

Wisdom Guidepost #10-Stir up Power Within You
2 Timothy 1:6-7

Therefore, I remind you to stir up the gift of God which is in you through the laying on of my hands. For God has not given us a spirit of fear, but of power and of love and of a sound mind.

There were times during my career I felt I had nothing left to give or not enough inner resources to do all required of me. Are you feeling or have felt the same way? Well, I have good news! You can handle every one of those tasks with excellence if you stir up the power (gifts) inside of you. If you don't let fear talk you out of it, you will find everything you need inside of you. Stir up your power! Inside of you is faith, power, and love. Say this out loud. "I stir up the power within me by my faith, and fear will not stop me. I'm stepping out on faith and expecting victory to follow me."

Paul, the writer of the Book of Timothy, wanted to cheer up the faint of heart and to inspire them with fresh courage to fight the "good fight of faith." For Paul knew that cowardice manifests itself by timidity, fear, and shrinking away from daily difficulties. But the Holy Spirit inside of you will give you the power, strength, and self-control to patiently endure and win over trials and temptations.

Wisdom Guidepost #11-Reality of Rejection
Isaiah 53: 3, 7

He is despised and rejected by men, A Man of sorrows and acquainted with grief. And we hid, as it were, our faces from Him; He was despised, and we did not esteem Him. He was oppressed and He was afflicted, Yet He opened not His mouth; He was led as a lamb to slaughter, And as a sheep before its shearers is silent, So He opened not His mouth.

Should we expect to be rejected? Does it come with the job?   Yes and yes! I know the sting of rejection, and I empathize with you if today you are feeling that pain too. The Prophet Isaiah paints a vivid picture of the rejection Jesus experienced, and yet He never said a word. Yeah, but can you be that strong? Surely you can! I remember the day I walked into a classroom with students who usually greeted me with warm greetings to a sea of silence and blank stares. I cringed with the dark emotion of rejection. I was shocked and confused. What had I done? What had changed? I carried out my classroom observation as usual; and later found out the teacher had spewed venom and lies into the minds of these impressionable teenagers in retaliation against me. You see, I had earlier dealt with the teacher about professional responsibilities. But instead of taking the correction as it was given—with compassion, the teacher coaxed the students into rejecting me. If you're in that dark place now, take a deep breath and release. I have good news—rejection is not a measure of your true worth. Don't agree with another person's evaluation of you, and don't wait for them to change. The problem is not yours, and the fault does not lie with you. Know your worth and continue to lead from the inside out!

Wisdom Guidepost #12-Sound of Criticism
I Peter 2:15

For this is the will of God, that by doing good you may put to silence the ignorance of foolish men.

W hen the sounds of criticism bombard your hearing, your natural response may be to silence it and strike back. Firing back is not the answer. Giving them a taste of their own medicine will only add fuel to the fire. So, what's the antidote? Continue to do good! Continue to speak the truth and lead with compassion. Criticism, like opposition and rejection are inevitable. But what makes the difference is how you react to them. Realize they are just distractions to take you off course and to steer you away from your vision. This is the day to go back to your office or workspace and re-read your vision. If you have a vision board stored away in a closet somewhere, pull it out and post it in a prominent area. Use your vision to re-ignite the passion for what you do. Remember your "why" --why you chose to be a compassionate leader or why you were called to lead. Either way, stay the course. In time the foolish words of your critics will dissipate, and you will still be standing strong.

Wisdom Guidepost #13- The Power to Create
Ephesians 5:1

Therefore, be imitators of God as dear children.

Compassionate leaders imagine the impossible. Curious and courageous are just two of the badges they wear. In her trainings, Margaret Wheatley, a management consultant who studies organizational behavior, introduced the mythical Shambhala warriors.

These warriors are simply people who wish to bring about great change and healing. Are these your aims? Are they included in your vision for the work you do? Then you are a Shambhala warrior…a visionary who uses compassion and insight to create the impossible. Compassion is essential because it motivates us to relieve the suffering of others. However, with compassion alone, leaders may fall short and become burned out, angry, or filled with despair. Insight and compassion together give structure to our warmth and imagination. Your passion, coupled with rational understanding of people and events around you and how they are interwoven, can be the genesis of creativity. Stop what you're doing! Breathe in and ask what is being asked of me now; and allow compassion and insight to guide your imagination. Follow through on these rational thoughts—not quick emotional decisions—and see clearly and act wisely to serve others. The environment you're in now may be chaotic but you don't have to be!

Wisdom Guidepost #14- Wired for Rest
Psalm 23:1-3

The Lord is my shepherd; I shall not want. He makes me to lie down in green pastures; He leads me beside the still waters. He restores my soul; He leads me in the paths of righteousness For His name's sake.

Y ou were created to lie down in green pastures of rest. But this electronic age keeps you 'wired' most of the time. At times you even feel guilty about turning off your phone or computer to spend a few moments in silence and peace. The culture of how things are done is fast and furious and then you collapse in exhaustion. This is not God's best for you. You have been called to walk beside still waters and paths of peace. It is here where your soul (mind, will and emotions) is refreshed, and your body is energized. Slow down, breathe in and exhale. You can be confident that whatever distressing situation is occupying your thoughts today will turn out okay when you commit your way to the Lord. The tasks you are charged with today do not have to be completed in a flash. Take a minute and connect with a trusted co-worker or companion, and your synergy will produce great results. Corey Booker, the first African American, U.S. Senator from New Jersey, gave this piece of advice during the 2020 Democratic National Convention. "If you want to go fast…go alone. If you want to go far…go together (based on African Proverb). Make rest a daily requirement, and you will go far fast.

Wisdom Guidepost #15- Be Silent...Listen
John 10:27-28

My sheep hear My voice, and I know them, and they follow Me. And I give them eternal life, and they shall never perish; neither shall anyone snatch them out of My hand.

Quietness is the classroom or boardroom where you learn to hear from the Creator. If you're at the Beginner's Level in hearing from the ever-present

Shepherd, you're going to need a quiet space to calm your mind and shut out the noise of your surroundings. As you become more disciplined in this process, you will carry this stillness with you throughout the day and wherever you go. At the Advanced Level, you will be skillful at listening to other people and the Creator. During the course of the day, you hear all kinds of conversations and commands thrown at you. There's the sound of music, traffic noise, sounds of nature, and self-talk. But at this level, the voice of the Creator is louder and leads you to make the right decisions. In your tranquil space, your body and mind relax, and you create a welcoming space for witty ideas, inventions, and confidence to overcome great obstacles. A great athlete takes time to prepare mentally before the race. Similarly, preparation equips you for the journey, so you don't grow weary and quit. Relax and listen—it is here where you receive wisdom from the Creator!

Dear God:
Enlighten what's dark in me …
Strengthen what's weak in me …
Mend what's broken in me …
Bind what's bruised in me …
Heal what's sick in me …
and lastly,
Revive whatever peace and
love has died in me.

Part 3 – Wisdom in Your Relationship with the Creator

Wisdom is not just about accumulating the right information; it is the ability to apply the truth to your life. Wisdom is like looking at life from a panoramic view and able to discern the proper next steps. This can be a formidable task if you try to do it alone. Let God be God in your life and trust Him in all things and walk in His path of truth. The psalmist prayed, "Teach me your way, O Lord, that I may walk in your truth (Psalm 86:11). I have found this is easy when times are good, but in difficult times I may tend to revert to worry and fear. Hear me clearly. Fear is the enemy of walking in truth. Fear as an acronym is:

F- False

E-Events

A-Appearing

R-Real

Even when you can't see the light at the end of the staircase, you must be willing to take the first step of faith in the Creator. He will lead you from darkness to light. It is my prayer that you will learn to walk by faith and not by sight (2 Corinthians 5:7). As a leader, you will always have to deal with difficult decisions and difficult people. But it is the posture you take in dealing with these situations that will mean the difference between victory or defeat. God will enter your battlefields before you-- The Creator wants you to win!

Through the years, I have learned to seek guidance from wise counselors like elders of the family, teachers, and mentors. But lately, I have discovered a deeper understanding and strength from the Spirit within. I am assured that I never have to walk in the darkness of doubt and fear. So, I turn within for that calm assurance that all is well. This calm assurance is not a license for me or for you, as a matter of fact, to use the Creator as a dumping ground. He expects us to do all we can in the natural, and He will do the supernatural. Let me interject this caveat here--God is not committed to your comfort, but He is committed to your character! Furthermore, wisdom teaches us not to deny the diagnosis but to defy the verdict. This can apply to a medical diagnosis (I know from personal experience), legal verdict, or anything spoken over your life.

Wisdom Guidepost #16-The Master Character Builder
Romans 5:1-4

Therefore, having been justified by faith, we have a peace with God through our Lord Jesus Christ, through whom also we have access by faith into this grace in which we stand, and rejoice in hope of the Glory of God. And not only that, but we also glory in tribulations, knowing that tribulation produces perseverance, and perseverance, character and character, hope.

Tribulation alone in Romans 5:4 does not bring about patience alone, but through the power of

God's grace working within you. And hope will not disappoint you when it is rooted, grounded, and sealed with the Spirit of love. Character, as defined by Merriam-Webster, is the mental and moral qualities distinctive to an individual. A story is told of a newly engaged couple who went to the movies, and the young man soon noticed what he believed was smoke coming from the movie screen. He immediately yelled fire and ran out of the theatre without ever noticing that his fiancé was not with him or if she were safely out. When he returned, he found her sitting there. The moral of the story is the fire did not cause the cowardice in his character, it only revealed it.

As a leader, let the dreamer be revealed in you. You should see yourself walking in the steps that lead to your summit of success. But beware, your climb will not come without great challenges. I'm reminded when I was positioned to move into principalship of the high school where I served as the Assistant and

Vice Principals, the sides started to "circle their wagons." One side said, "We've never promoted from within." The other side said, "There are only one or two female high school principals." Both sides were convinced I would not be the committee's selection. But none of that phased me—I maintained my character of diplomacy and hope. I did not let the fear of being rejected overcome me. Today, will you maintain your authentic character in the face of attack? I want you to hold on to who you are—a confident, compassionate leader. Fear of failure or attack is a dangerous emotion. But know this emotion is just a shadow as Paul wrote in Psalm 23:4—As I walk through the shadow of death, I will fear no evil.

Hold fast to your dreams. Write them down and share them with your mentor or trusted companion. Some visual learners may want to construct a vision board and lay out each step and monitor it as each comes to fruition. Persevere and don't let go. No matter how tight troops circle their wagons, keep your eyes on the summit where dreams come true.

"Too many of us are not living our dreams because we are living our fears."
(Les Brown)

Wisdom Guidepost #17-Wait Patiently
Hebrews 6:12

That you do not become sluggish, but imitate those who through faith and patience inherit the promises.

Faith and endurance, some may say, sound like a lot of work. In these times of instant breakfast, a career in a year, and Marriage at First Sight, patience is a hard sale. I offer you the advice of Dr. Norman Vincent Peale, who said, "Through enthusiasm, prayer and faith, you can reach your highest goals. To make your dreams come true, 'Ask and believe; dream and believe; work and believe." Today you may be feeling you're at the end of your rope. You've dealt with the same issues for years, and they stubbornly plague you. Strategies purported by experts in the faith community and in business and education have failed to yield results, and you're tempted to give up. Don't! Hold on and allow patience to bolster your faith until the resolutions manifest. Patience is power, and it overpowers fear. Refuse to draw back or lose confidence. Patience in the Bible is seen as the ability to stand fast on the Word of God, even when success is slow in coming. Patience is not automatic, and Peter Drucker, management consultant, educator, and author whose writings contributed to the foundations for modern business corporations, said, "Nothing good happens by accident...put some structure around it." Use this waiting period to build a structure around your vision and hold on until you're on the other side!

Wisdom Guidepost #18- Humility & Empathy
Ruth 3:11

And now, my daughter, do not fear. I will do for you all that you request, for all the people of my town know that you are a virtuous woman.

Yes, I know many don't like labels; and the term "virtuous" is not used commonly in the present culture. Some may even think it's hackneyed or outdated. Let's read how Jesus used "virtue" in Luke

8:46. And Jesus said, "Somebody hath touched me for I perceive that virtue is gone out of me. Here virtue is the power to do the right thing in any given situation. That power is at the root of character, forming a personality where its habits tend towards doing the right thing. I ask you this question, "Do you want to be en vogue or successful? Compassionate leaders exemplify humility and empathy. When we do, we run the risk of being viewed as "soft." But I ask you to reflect on God's words to Ruth—don't worry, I will do what is necessary, for everyone knows you are a virtuous woman. I'd like to apply this wisdom to the challenge you may be dealing with today. "Don't worry about what those who do not matter are saying. The ones that matter know your character and know you are a powerful, compassionate leader. Your worth and character are not determined by the challenge you are dealing with at this moment. Your character is rooted and grounded in doing the right thing, regardless of others' perceptions and opinions. Don't waste time on the opinion of those who do not matter.

Expect tension but be clear and certain to remain true to your values and your vision. Don't become apathetic or lose hope. Apathy leads to a frozen will and vision. Don't let it happen! God will do what's necessary for you to win!

Your character is rooted and grounded in doing the right thing, regardless of others' perceptions and opinions.

Wisdom Guidepost #19 - Passing the Test: Your Back is Covered Jeremiah 17:7-8

Blessed is the man who trusts in the Lord, And whose hope is the Lord. For he shall be like a tree planted by the waters, Which spreads out its roots by the river, And will not fear when heat comes; But its leaf will be green, And will not be anxious in the year of drought, Nor will cease from yielding fruit.

As of today, Saturday, February 23, 2021, national news reported over 200,000 lives have been lost in the United States due to the coronavirus. Many died alone in hospitals and nursing homes without the presence of family or friends. I must admit these are dark times for all of us. There are trials before us, and we wonder how we will ever overcome them. We search our arsenal of strategies that worked in the past and found them ineffective for this season. We talk with trusted confidantes and dependable elders of your families, only to hear them say, "I've never seen anything like this." These trials don't stop at attacks on your health and well-being. They invade your professional lives as well. Are you feeling alone and exposed to a harsh winter day without a coat? Have those who started a project with you withdrawn their support for no apparent reason? I know this uncomfortable feeling so well; and have asked, "Does anyone have my back"? The Prophet Jeremiah answered that question and assures us that God's got our back—He is our rear and front guard. He's there for you and ready to lead you through troubled waters.

So, let Him help you—release it all to Him; and listen for His still, quiet voice of wisdom and guidance. Right now, take time to breathe and pray. Soon you will see your prayers answered and spirit, soul, and body renewed! He is your lighthouse… lighting the way!

Wisdom Guidepost #20 -Were You Called to do This or Not? Ephesians 1:18

The eyes of your understanding being enlightened; that you may know what is the hope of His calling, what are the riches of His inheritance in the saints.

D o you feel today is one of those days you left your confident self at home? Are you questioning every decision you've made? Compassionate leaders are reflective in their practice. Donald Schon was a philosopher and professor in Urban Planning at the Massachusetts Institute of Technology (MIT). He defined reflective practice as the ability to reflect on one's actions to engage in the process of continuous learning and developmental insight. Reflective practice can help you develop creative thinking skills and encourages active engagement in work processes. I want you to know you were built for what you're doing. Stop letting doubt and fear rob you of the confident hope God has given when He called you to do what you are doing right now. He has promised you a rich inheritance. The great thing about inheritance is we get it whether we deserve it or not. If it's promised to you in writing—it's yours. The written record is in the Word of God (the Bible). You've got to stand in confidence and believe you were called to win and to help others to win alongside of you. Compassionate leaders exemplify the win/win attitude daily. You were built to do the hard things, so sharpen your skills and gifts and believe in yourself. Wisdom is knowing your career is what you are paid to do, but your calling is what you were made to do.

"Compassionate leaders exemplify
the win/win attitude daily."

Wisdom Guidepost #21 – Who are You Tethered to?
Romans 12:2

And do not be conformed to this world, but be transformed by the renewing of your mind, that you may prove what is that good and acceptable and perfect will of God.

When you consider the hectic, complex life you live, it's no wonder you may feel drained and confused. The lighthouse, the symbol for this book, is a reminder you are not alone. It stands as a guide for those traveling the sea. A ship tethered to the shore floats securely though it may rock back and forth by the force of the winds and waves. But it's protected and won't crash into the rocks or get lost at sea. Compassionate leaders are like that ship. What you are experiencing or feeling today may have you feeling battered or lost, but that's a lie—an untruth. You, too, are securely tethered to God and anchored in His protection and wisdom. You can handle whatever presents itself today when you are centered in The Power Higher than Yourself. Fear must flee, and you are free to think clearly and make wise decisions. You must be willing to abandon thought processes that no longer serve you and submit to being transformed from the inside out. You may have to stop leading like others lead and chart your own course—knowing you are tethered to Spirit. You must change how you think with a renewed mind that is centered on God's will for your life. You've got this, and you are as strong and sturdy as the lighthouse!

Wisdom Guidepost #22 – Live Your Best Life & Make the Greatest Impact
Habakkuk 3:17-18

Though the fig tree may not blossom, Nor fruit be on the vines; Though the labor of the olive may fail, And the fields yield no food; Though the flock may cut off from the fold, And there be no herd in the stalls—Yet I will rejoice in the Lord, I will joy in the God of my salvation.

Joy is more than a warm, happy feeling that comes when things around you are going well. Joy is not dependent on your circumstances. It is a powerful force from which you can lead with compassion. True Joy is found in the serene presence of Spirit. So, you can experience it in the classroom, boardroom, or on a crowded subway. Don't rule Joy out because your day is filled with difficulties. Joy does her best work in circumstances like that. Remember you're tethered to Some-one greater than these temporary distractions. Concentrate on the truth you know—you can handle this—you are wise and strong. Know that most of what you worry about doesn't happen, and the others will work themselves out. No matter what circumstances you are facing today, you can be filled with Joy. Lead from your heart—from the inside out, and you will win!

Rejoice and be proud of the work you do, the person you are, and the difference you make! Be your best self so you can make the greatest impact!

Wisdom Guidepost #23 – Complete What He Started Philippians 1:6

Being confident of this very thing, that He who has begun a good work in you will complete it until the day of Jesus Christ.

I can't count the times I've started and stopped writing this book. I allowed people and things to take me off course. At the time, I deemed them more important than fulfilling my dream of publishing this wisdom manual on leadership. One of those detours was a cancer diagnosis. You will never hear me say, "I had cancer," because I realize the power of my words. I didn't deny the diagnosis, but I defied the verdict. So, in October 2018, when I was diagnosed with an aggressive form of breast cancer, I put down my pen and walked away from my book. Today, I am healed, whole and well. The man-made tests, namely the mammogram and sonogram confirm it! I am finishing what God started in me and will not stop until these wisdom guides are in the hands of compassionate leaders like you. What have you started and stopped? What projects have you started and not finished that you know would bless others? It's never too late to begin again! Don't condemn yourself—give yourself a good dose of Grace. You know how to do it. All compassionate leaders are quick to grace others. Today, it's your turn to be on the receiving end. What is it that God has been trying to birth in you? Birthing those things in our spirit is tantamount to birthing a child.

Labor is a natural process, and every person's birthing process is unique. Sometimes labor is over in a matter of hours; and for others, it may take much longer. Birthing your gift to others can be physically and emotionally draining. It takes stamina, but you were built for this. Keep showing up--endure until your project come forth!

P – Push

U - Until

S - Something

H - Happens

In This House …
We are real
We make mistakes
We say I'm sorry
We give second chances
We have fun
We forgive
We share laughter
We chase dreams
We love …
Anonymous

Part 4 – Wisdom in Your Family

I share these words published in Langston Hughes's first collection of poetry, The Weary Blues in 1926. This poem, Mother to Son, chronicles the lives of African Americans who struggle against the woes of life—like poverty and discrimination.

"Well, son, I'll tell you:

Life for me ain't been no crystal stair.

I's had tacks in it,

And splinters,

And boards torn up,

And places with no carpet on the floor –

Bare.

But all the time I'se been a-climbin' on,

And reaching' landin's,

And turn' corners,

And sometimes goin' in the dark

Where there ain't been no light.

So boy, don't you turn back.

Don't you set down on the steps

'Cause you finds it's kinder hard.

Don't you fall now –

For I'se still goin', honey,

I'se still climbin',

And life for me ain't been no crystal stair."

--Langston Hughes

It takes courage to conquer the woes of life that come against you and your family. Today you may feel defeated and low on Hope. But Mother Wisdom is quietly saying, put your problems in perspective," When trials and trouble weigh you down like a ship's anchor—trust God. He will be a lighthouse in the dark times for you and your family. Then remind yourself to keep focused on your goals and plans in the weeks and months ahead. Today, what seems insurmountable will be resolved and forgotten. Keep on climbing!

Wisdom Guidepost #24 – Be Courageous
Deuteronomy 31:6

"Be strong and of good courage, do not fear nor be afraid of them; for the Lord your God, He is the One who goes with you. He will not leave you nor forsake you."

Dr. Maya Angelou said, "Courage is the most important of all virtues because without courage you cannot practice any other virtue consistently. You can practice virtue erratically, but nothing consistently without courage." Life is full of situations where you are faced with uncertainty. Even though you have goals to achieve, the fear of the unknown can potentially hold you back from following your dreams. Like me, I know you have dreams for your family. As you move through this day, keep in mind God's Word, and let Him guide you. God is asking you to not fear, to be of good cheer, and to be courageous (Joshua 1:9). I've learned and passed it on to you—It is natural to be afraid, but it is detrimental to your physical and spiritual health to live in constant fear!

Wisdom Guidepost #25 – Power of Love
I Corinthians 16:13, 14

Watch, stand fast in the faith, be brave, be strong.
Let all that you do be done with love.

L ove is one thing that unites you with others in your life. It can inspire, encourage, and lighten our hearts. Love of a significant other during times of trouble can be that ray of light to lead you out of a dark place. Love can be confusing too. The Bible has a lot to say about Love: Love is patient and kind. Love is not jealous or boastful or proud or rude. It does not demand its own way. It is not easily provoked. It is not irritable, and it keeps no record of being wrong. It does not rejoice about injustices but rejoices whenever the truth wins out. Love never gives us, never loses faith is always hopeful, and endures through every circumstance (I Corinthians 13:4-7). Wow! This is the resume for a compassionate leader like you. Make this a checklist for yourself and refer to it often. Continue to lead your family from the inside out and do everything with Love. In Celine Dion's song, The Power of Love, she says she feels lost, but is ready to learn the power of Love. These words may capture how you're feeling right now. Know that Love can assuage this discomfort. Love, like the lighthouse, can guide you to safe harbor!

.

Wisdom Guidepost #26 – Grace Yourself
Romans 3:23-24

For all have sinned and fall short of the glory of God, being justified freely by His grace through the redemption that is in Christ Jesus.

E ver sat alone in the room after a Board Meeting where your presentation was picked apart—piece by piece? Ever failed to contribute your usual level of excellence to a group project? How did you feel? Pretty lousy—right? Okay, how did you feel when you forgot the birthday of your significant other or best friend or said a coarse word to one of your children? Stop! Enough! I know you don't want to be reminded; but listen to these words of wisdom from Les Brown, an international motivational speaker.

"Give yourself a break. Stop beating yourself up! Everyone makes mistakes, has setbacks and failures. You don't come with a book on how to get it right all the time. You will fail sometimes, not because you planned to, but simply because you're human. Failure is part of creating a great life. Stand up to it and handle it with Grace--because you can." The world tells you to do better, be better, and hustle more. These commands pressure you to believe you must have it all together. When you make a mistake, you may begin negative self-talk that profits you nothing. Instead, you need to give yourself Grace. God freely gives you

Grace, so agree with Him by doing the same. Look into the past, and see the times your significant other, best friend, or child disappointed or failed you. I'm sure you forgave them and moved forward. You were gracious, kind, and forgiving. Today, grace yourself—you deserve it. After all, God calls you His Beloved (3 John 2). When you make a mistake or blunder, let it go, shift your thoughts forward, persevere, and succeed. Move on with wisdom knowing there is no going forward without the Creator, and with Him, there is no turning back!

Wisdom Guidepost #27 – Pray for Others
I Timothy 2:1-2

Therefore, I exhort first of all that supplications, prayers intercession, and giving of thanks be made to all men, for kings and all who are in authority that we may lead a quiet and peaceable life in all godliness and reverence.

I once read, can't remember where, that prayer is the bridge between panic and peace. I've learned the painful lesson that we teach others how to treat us. This is true for those related to you by blood and those in your sphere of influence. Family-- love them or love them not—either way, some can be difficult individuals. I don't believe difficult people were born that way. Fear and search for safety can drive them to respond in a hurtful, unwelcomed manner. Are you feeling the sting of pain from the dart of a family member today? It's family, so you can't simply end the relationship. You've tried in the past to not take it personally. You've had the critical conversation and set boundaries, but the boundaries keep being crossed or blurred. There may be little you can do to change this behavior, but Wisdom says, "You can change the way you let it affect you." Compassion is the most empowering choice that leads you to pray for your family. Hold steadily in prayer and give the person time to work through whatever is at the root of the behavior. Remember, you are in control of your behavior. Leading from the heart will be uncomfortable, but prayer is your powerful weapon to bring harmony to your familial relationships. As you grow and apply these wisdom guideposts, you will realize the transcript of your prayers become the script for your life.

"Remember, you are in control of your behavior."

Wisdom Guidepost #28 – Balance Home and Work
Philippians 4:8

Finally, brethren, whatever things are true, whatever
things are noble, whatever things are just, whatever
things are pure, whatever things are lovely, whatever
things are of good report, if there is any virtue and if
there is anything praiseworthy meditate on these things.

It's 6:15 PM, and you're still at work. What self-talk
are you having? "Life is not fair. I have personal
goals; we have family goals, and I'm trying to achieve

them both. But to do so, I have to sacrifice time with my family." You view overtime as a vehicle to financial freedom, but sometimes your family doesn't understand. And you may be experiencing feelings of guilt and condemnation. Stop! Yes, you must manage your time well. Yes, you must find that balance between home and work. But in the process, there is no need to be hard on yourself or your family. As a single parent with two sons, it was a challenge to find this balance. My negative self-talk did not benefit me at home nor work. Compassionate leaders come to realize the quality of the time trumps the quantity. This is not a trite statement—it is the truth based in wisdom. This equilibrium will come if you focus your attention and thoughts on things that are pure and worthy of praise. Your family will navigate through these challenging times and become more understanding and thankful for your sacrifice and dedication. I feel a little humor is needed right about now: Problems are like washing machines. They twist, they spin, & knock us around. But in the end, we come out cleaner, brighter &

better than ever! "But remember and never forget—You can be replaced at work but not at home!"

"Compassionate leaders come to realize the quality of the time trumps the quantity."

'There is no magic wand that can resolve our problems. The solution rests with our work and discipline."

-Jose Eduardo dos Santos

Wisdom Guidepost #29 – Discipline the Family
Proverbs 1:8 & I Peter 3:7

My son, hear the instruction of your father. And do not forsake the law of your mother.

&

Husbands, likewise, dwell with them with understanding, giving honor to the wife, as to the weaker vessel, and a being heirs together of the grace of life, that your prayers may not be hindered.

It has been said that a man's home is his castle, but what happens when discipline is lacking? As a principal, I witnessed peace being overridden by chaos in the environment of my students. Our children, I believe, are a blessing from God. Today may be one of those days where it's a stretch to view them in this light. Your voice seems to be muffled by the noise of electronic devices and posts on social media. In your home, discipline may seem like a foreign concept and can't be found anywhere in the house. Are you looking for a safe harbor—a place of peace and mutual respect? A place where children are obedient to parents, the husband deals respectfully with his wife, and the wife regards the husband as the headship of the family. Stand with confidence in your position and firmly call each person to the task with the same compassion you give those in the workplace, Church, or community. Healthy discipline teaches everyone how to get their needs met. It also teaches problem-solving and self-control. When family members test their boundaries and your nerves, remind them the purpose of boundaries is to keep them safe in a nurturing environment. Stand your ground and be the compassionate leader for your family!

"Stand with confidence in your position and firmly call each person to the task with compassion."

Wisdom Source #30 – Start Again— Go back to #1 2 Corinthians 5:17

Therefore, if anyone is in Christ, he is a new creation; old things have passed away; behold all things have become new.

The journey of a lifetime starts with the turn of this page. New beginnings are awaiting you and those you love every day. Begin from the beginning of these wisdom guideposts and experience the Joy of leading from the inside out. Being a compassionate leader is worth it all, and it has its reward. I honor you and pray you never stop giving Grace and gracing yourself. Finish well, for I believe we are at the vanguard of a better world with compassionate leaders like you and me at the helm!

Shalom

Dr. Val

dr.valrhoden@gmail.com

Reflective Journal Entries

"Life can only be understood backwards;

but it must be lived forwards.

Soren Kierkegaard

Journaling is keeping a record of occurrences, expressions, or observations. Use these pages to write reflective journal entries detailing your private thoughts and feelings. May the 30 wisdom guideposts in this wisdom manual inspire you to journal daily to help heal your compassionate heart and inspire you to continue to lead from the inside out!

Day: _Monday_

Date: _5_ / _3_ / _21_

Occurrences, Expressions, or Observations

The Month of May!
Spring forth today
Rejoice and be glad! ♡ ♪

Day: _____

Date: ___ / ___ / ___

Occurrences,   Expressions,   or   Observations

_____
_____
_____
_____
_____
_____
_____
_____
_____
_____
_____
_____
_____
_____
_____
_____

Day: _____

Date: ___ / ___ / ___

Occurrences, Expressions, or Observations

_____

_____

_____

_____

_____

_____

_____

_____

_____

_____

_____

_____

_____

_____

_____

_____

Day: _____

Date: ___ / ___ / ___

Occurrences,   Expressions,   or   Observations

_____

_____

_____

_____

_____

_____

_____

_____

_____

_____

_____

_____

_____

_____

_____

Day: _____

Date: ___ / ___ / ___

Occurrences,   Expressions,   or   Observations

_____

_____

_____

_____

_____

_____

_____

_____

_____

_____

_____

_____

_____

_____

_____

_____

Day: _____

Date: ___ / ___ / ___

Occurrences,   Expressions,   or   Observations

_____

_____

_____

_____

_____

_____

_____

_____

_____

_____

_____

_____

_____

_____

_____

_____

Day: _____

Date: ___ / ___ / ___

Occurrences, Expressions, or Observations

_____

_____

_____

_____

_____

_____

_____

_____

_____

_____

_____

_____

_____

_____

_____

_____

_____

Day: _____

Date: ___ / ___ / ___

Occurrences, Expressions, or Observations

_____

_____

_____

_____

_____

_____

_____

_____

_____

_____

_____

_____

_____

_____

_____

_____

_____

Day: _____

Date: ___ / ___ / ___

Occurrences,   Expressions,   or   Observations

_____

_____

_____

_____

_____

_____

_____

_____

_____

_____

_____

_____

_____

_____

_____

_____

Day: _____

Date: ___ / ___ / ___

Occurrences, Expressions, or Observations

_____

_____

_____

_____

_____

_____

_____

_____

_____

_____

_____

_____

_____

_____

_____

_____

Day: _____

Date: ___ / ___ / ___

Occurrences,   Expressions,   or   Observations

_____

_____

_____

_____

_____

_____

_____

_____

_____

_____

_____

_____

_____

_____

_____

_____

Day: _____

Date: ___ / ___ / ___

Occurrences, Expressions, or Observations

_____

_____

_____

_____

_____

_____

_____

_____

_____

_____

_____

_____

_____

_____

_____

_____

Day: _____

Date: ___ / ___ / ___

Occurrences,   Expressions,   or   Observations

_____

_____

_____

_____

_____

_____

_____

_____

_____

_____

_____

_____

_____

_____

_____

Day: _____

Date: ___ / ___ / ___

Occurrences, Expressions, or Observations

_____

_____

_____

_____

_____

_____

_____

_____

_____

_____

_____

_____

_____

_____

_____

_____

Day: _____

Date: ___ / ___ / ___

Occurrences, Expressions, or Observations

_____
_____
_____
_____
_____
_____
_____
_____
_____
_____
_____
_____
_____
_____
_____
_____
_____

Day: _____

Date: ___ / ___ / ___

Occurrences, Expressions, or Observations

_____

_____

_____

_____

_____

_____

_____

_____

_____

_____

_____

_____

_____

_____

_____

_____

_____

_____

Day: _____

Date: ___ / ___ / ___

Occurrences, Expressions, or Observations

_____

_____

_____

_____

_____

_____

_____

_____

_____

_____

_____

_____

_____

_____

_____

_____

_____

Day: _____

Date: ___ / ___ / ___

Occurrences, Expressions, or Observations

_____

_____

_____

_____

_____

_____

_____

_____

_____

_____

_____

_____

_____

_____

_____

_____

Day: _____

Date: ___ / ___ / ___

Occurrences,   Expressions,   or   Observations

_____

_____

_____

_____

_____

_____

_____

_____

_____

_____

_____

_____

_____

_____

_____

_____

Day: _____

Date: ___ / ___ / ___

Occurrences,   Expressions,   or   Observations

_____

_____

_____

_____

_____

_____

_____

_____

_____

_____

_____

_____

_____

_____

_____

_____

This is my Declaration of Faith for all who read these words and recorded their occurrences, expressions, or observations:

"Now may God, the inspiration and fountain of hope, fill you to overflowing with uncontainable joy and perfect peace as you trust in him. And may the power of the Holy Spirit continually surround your life with his super-abundance until you radiate with hope!"

Romans 15:13 (The Passion Translation)

Made in the USA
Columbia, SC
15 April 2021